MONSTER 123s

Written by Tim and Barb Read

Illustrated by Tim Read

For Mom.
Thanks for the crayons.
-T.R.

For Tim, the most creative,
inspiring, and silliest monster I know.
Thank you for sharing this life with me.
- B.R.

Text copyright © 2013 Tim Read · Illustration copyright © 2013 Tim Read

ISBN-13: 978-1490314112   ISBN-10: 1490314113

Visit us at:
www.MyVerySillyMonster.com

One

Wally's

Watermelon

Two

Tina's

Tulips

BEST THUMBS
CONTEST

Three

Theo's

Thumbs

Four

Fanny's

Fangs

Five

Finn's

Fish

Six

Sam's

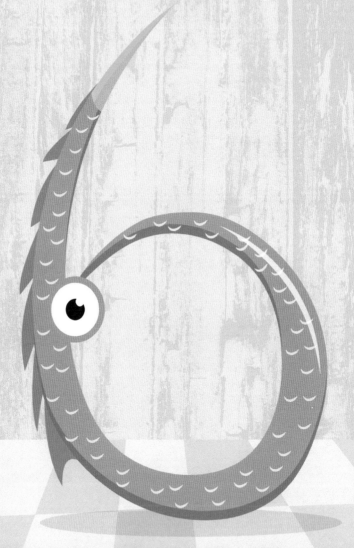

Sandwiches

Seven

Sally's

Sisters

Eight

Avery's

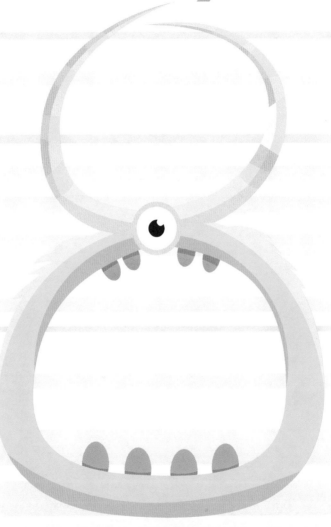

Acorns

Nine

Newton's

Noses

Ten

Tilly's

Turtles

Eleven

Eli's

Eyes

Twilla's

12

Twigs

13

Thirteen

Thelma's

Thorns

Fourteen

Floyd's

Forks

Fifteen

Fergie's

15

Figs

Sixteen

Sigmond's

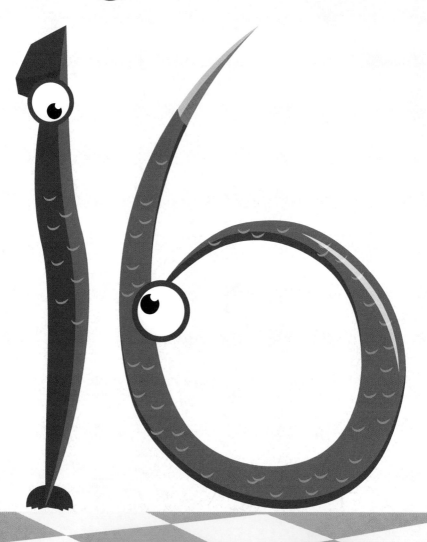

Slugs

Seventeen

Sven's

Seahorses

Eighteen

Angus's

Angels

Nineteen

Nick's

19

Nails

Twenty

Ted's

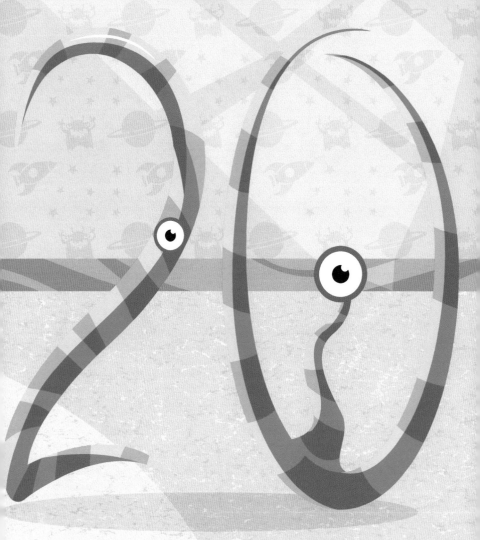

Tops

Also available from

MY VERY SILLY MONSTER

Made in the USA
Lexington, KY
13 September 2013